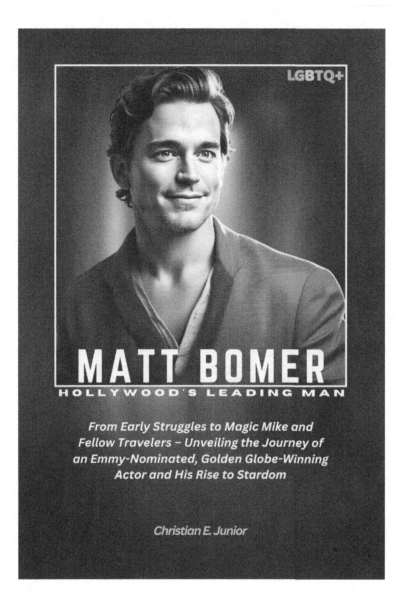

MATT BOMER
HOLLYWOOD'S LEADING MAN

From Early Struggles to Magic Mike and Fellow Travelers – Unveiling the Journey of an Emmy-Nominated, Golden Globe-Winning Actor and His Rise to Stardom

Christian E. Junior

Copyright © Christian E. Junior 2025

All rights reserved. No part of this publication may be reproduced, distributed, or transmitted in any form or by any means, including photocopying, recording, or other electronic or mechanical methods, without the prior written permission of the publisher, except in the case of brief quotations embodied in critical reviews and certain other noncommercial uses permitted by copyright law.

DEDICATION

To those who dare to dream and stay true to themselves, your journey is the greatest story of all.

To Matt, for showing us that authenticity is the key to greatness.

FOREWORD

In an industry that often demands conformity, Matt Bomer has stood out not only for his talent but for his unwavering commitment to authenticity.

This biography explores more than just his impressive career, it unveils the heart of a man who has used his platform to make a lasting impact. From his early struggles to his rise as a leading man in Hollywood, Matt's story is a testament to perseverance, passion, and the power of living your truth.

This book is an invitation to dive deeper into the man behind the roles, to explore the journeys of personal growth and advocacy, and to reflect on the legacy he continues to build both on and off the screen.

ACKNOWLEDGEMENT

I'd like to extend my deepest gratitude to Matt Bomer for being a constant source of inspiration. His openness and courage made this journey possible, and I'm honored to share his story.

A special thank you to the many colleagues, friends, and mentors who've supported Matt through his career, your words and experiences have added so much depth to this book.

To my team, thank you for your unwavering support in bringing this story to life.

And finally, to the readers, thank you for taking the time to learn more about a man whose story continues to inspire. Your belief in authenticity makes all the difference.

ABOUT THE AUTHOR

Christian E. Junior is a writer, author, and avid storyteller with a passion for bringing compelling, real-life stories to the page. With a deep interest in exploring the lives of cultural icons, Christian works focus on those who have made lasting impressions through their talents, values, and personal journeys. In addition to writing biographies, he is dedicated to crafting stories that inspire and empower readers. When not writing, Christian enjoys reading, traveling, and connecting with the vibrant communities that fuel his creativity.

Table of Content

Copyright © Christian E. Junior 2025.................. 3
DEDICATION.. 4
FOREWORD... 5
ACKNOWLEDGEMENT.................................. 6
ABOUT THE AUTHOR.................................... 7
INTRODUCTION... 10

CHAPTER ONE... 17
    EARLY LIFE – FROM WEBSTER GROVES TO HOLLYWOOD DREAMS

CHAPTER TWO... 25
    THE ROAD TO FAME – STRUGGLES AND BREAKTHROUGHS

CHAPTER THREE.. 33
    MAGIC MIKE AND THE TRANSFORMATION

CHAPTER FOUR... 40
    FELLOW TRAVELERS AND THE NEW HORIZONS OF HIS CAREER

CHAPTER FIVE... 48
    AWARDS AND RECOGNITION – THE CRITICAL ACCLAIM

CHAPTER SIX... 55
    PERSONAL LIFE – THE MAN BEHIND THE

ACTOR

CHAPTER SEVEN 63
ADVOCACY AND PHILANTHROPY – GIVING BACK TO THE COMMUNITY

CHAPTER EIGHT 71
NAVIGATING THE FAME – BALANCING HOLLYWOOD'S DEMANDS WITH PERSONAL VALUES

CHAPTER NINE 78
THE FUTURE – CONTINUING TO EVOLVE AS AN ACTOR AND HUMAN BEING

CONCLUSION 85
A LEGACY OF PASSION, TALENT, AND AUTHENTICITY

BONUS 92

INTRODUCTION

Matt Bomer's journey to becoming one of Hollywood's most respected and versatile actors is not a story of overnight success, but one built on years of hard work, dedication, and passion. Born in Webster Groves, Missouri, Matt grew up with dreams of making it big in the world of entertainment. But, like many others before him, his path to Hollywood fame was anything but easy. It was shaped by personal struggles, professional setbacks, and the unwavering desire to make his mark in the industry he loved.

Today, Matt Bomer stands as a Hollywood leading man. His career achievements speak for themselves: an Emmy nomination for his role in "The Normal Heart", a Golden Globe win for his portrayal of a man battling AIDS in "The Normal Heart", and unforgettable performances in "Magic Mike" and "Fellow Travelers". But behind the accolades and the fame lies a story of resilience, of a man who never gave up, even when the odds were stacked against him. In this biography, we delve into both the professional milestones and the personal experiences that have shaped Matt's journey.

From his early days growing up in a quiet suburban town to becoming an international star, this biography explores the moments that defined Matt's life. His family, his values, and his determination to succeed shaped who he is today. But so did the struggles, his early days in New York City, where he faced rejection after rejection. He was not the typical "Hollywood" type. He didn't come from a long line of famous actors or wealthy families. Instead, Matt's determination came from within, a drive to prove himself, not only as a performer but as a person who could rise above his circumstances and make his dreams come true.

The first section of this biography will take readers back to Matt's roots, giving an in-depth look at his upbringing and the early influences that sparked his passion for acting. Raised in a supportive family, Matt was encouraged to explore his interests. His parents, while not in the entertainment industry themselves, fostered an environment that valued creativity and hard work. As a young boy, Matt was drawn to the arts, particularly theater, and found a sense of belonging in school performances and community theater groups. Little did he know, these early steps would set him on a path that would eventually lead him to the bright lights of Hollywood.

As he grew older, Matt realized that his passion for acting wasn't just a childhood hobby, it was a calling. At the age of 18, he left Missouri for New York City to pursue his dreams of becoming an actor. However, the reality of the entertainment industry quickly set in. New York City, with its glitz and glamor, also had a harsh reality for young actors. Rejection, tough auditions, and financial struggles were common challenges. But Matt's persistence pushed him forward. He worked tirelessly, refining his craft, attending classes, and auditioning for any role that could get him a foot in the door. He wasn't discouraged by the early setbacks. Instead, he embraced them, knowing each audition, each rejection, brought him closer to the success he sought.

After years of hard work, Matt finally landed his breakthrough role in the soap opera "Guiding Light". This was the moment that signaled a shift in his career. But it wasn't just about the role itself, it was about the recognition of his potential, the acknowledgment that he was no longer just an aspiring actor; he was someone with undeniable talent. "Guiding Light" gave him the visibility he needed to attract bigger roles, and soon, Matt was appearing in guest spots on shows like "Chuck" and "Supernatural".

But it wasn't until his role in "Magic Mike" that Matt truly began to gain the widespread recognition that would catapult him into Hollywood's A-list. As the charming and charismatic male stripper, Matt showcased a side of himself that audiences had never seen before. His portrayal in "Magic Mike" solidified him as more than just a pretty face, he was a skilled actor with depth and presence. And while the role may have been physically demanding, it was also a pivotal moment in his career that introduced him to a global audience. It was the start of a new chapter, one where he would no longer be confined to certain roles, but where he could expand into more diverse and complex characters.

Matt's success continued to grow with notable roles in films like "The Nice Guys" and "The Magnificent Seven". His acting range became even more evident as he moved seamlessly between comedic and dramatic roles. Yet, it was his role in "The Normal Heart" that would mark one of the most significant milestones of his career. Playing a man living with AIDS during the early years of the epidemic, Matt's portrayal of Felix Turner was raw, powerful, and heart-wrenching. It earned him critical acclaim and an Emmy nomination for Outstanding Supporting Actor in a Limited Series. The role was not just a career-defining moment, it was a deeply personal experience, one that gave him the opportunity to raise awareness about the AIDS crisis while showcasing his immense acting talent.

But despite his rising fame, Matt has always managed to keep a sense of humility and authenticity. He never let his success define who he was as a person. Instead, he remained grounded, always prioritizing his family, his personal values, and his commitment to giving back. His advocacy work especially within the LGBTQ+ community has been a major part of his life outside of acting. Matt has been open about his sexuality and the importance of visibility in Hollywood, using his platform to create change and promote inclusivity.

In this biography, readers will learn not only about Matt's career but also about his personal growth. The story behind his rise to fame is just as compelling as his professional achievements. Matt has faced numerous challenges, from navigating the pressures of Hollywood to confronting personal struggles and finding balance in a world that often seems to demand more than anyone can give. Through it all, he has remained true to himself, an actor, a husband, a father, and a man committed to making a difference in the world.

As you read this biography, you will uncover the untold stories of Matt Bomer's journey, his beginnings, his battles, his triumphs, and the ongoing evolution of his career. You will come to understand the man behind the roles, someone who has consistently pushed boundaries, embraced new challenges, and carved out a place for himself in Hollywood. His story is one of perseverance, passion, and authenticity, a story that will inspire anyone who has ever dreamed of rising above adversity to achieve their goals.

CHAPTER ONE

EARLY LIFE – FROM WEBSTER GROVES TO HOLLYWOOD DREAMS

Matt Bomer's story begins not in the bright lights of Hollywood, but in the quiet suburban town of Webster Groves, Missouri, where he was born on October 11, 1977. In many ways, his early life was far removed from the world of celebrity and fame. Yet, even in these formative years, the foundation for his future was being laid not just in terms of talent and ambition, but in the values instilled by his family, the community he grew up in, and the early lessons that would guide him throughout his life.

Matt was born into a family that encouraged him to explore his passions and follow his heart. His mother, a former school district worker, and his father, a successful writer and former executive at a private telecommunications firm, were both supportive of his aspirations, even when the idea of an acting career seemed out of reach. His family's influence was key in shaping Matt's confidence, work ethic, and resilience, traits that would later prove essential as he navigated the challenges of Hollywood.

Growing up in Webster Groves, a small, tight-knit community in St. Louis County, Matt was surrounded by the stability and encouragement that comes from a strong family foundation. His parents taught him the importance of education, hard work, and persistence, values that would become his guiding principles. Though they weren't in the entertainment industry, they recognized and nurtured Matt's early passion for performance. His mother, in particular, played a vital role in fostering his love for the arts, often taking him to local theater productions and enrolling him in community programs. She encouraged him to pursue his interests, offering her unwavering support as he honed his skills.

Matt was introduced to the world of theater at a young age, and it quickly became clear that he had a natural talent for acting. Whether it was performing in school plays or local productions, he was drawn to the stage. It was here that he first experienced the magic of storytelling, and the connection between the actor and the audience. At just 10 years old, he had already discovered that acting wasn't just a hobby, it was something he was meant to do. His performances were known for their authenticity, and he quickly earned the respect of those around him.

But it wasn't just his acting talent that stood out, it was his determination. Even at a young age, Matt showed the kind of tenacity and commitment that would become his hallmark as he moved through life. He was dedicated to his craft, constantly seeking out opportunities to learn, grow, and challenge himself. Whether it was participating in school drama clubs or seeking out summer theater camps, Matt always found ways to keep improving and perfecting his skills. This was the beginning of the work ethic that would fuel his rise to stardom.

Matt's childhood was marked by influences both inside and outside his family that helped shape his character. Growing up in the Midwest, he was exposed to a strong sense of community, hard work, and humility, qualities that he would carry with him throughout his life and career. His parents were pillars of the community, and their example of professionalism and dedication rubbed off on him. They taught him the importance of balance of being focused and determined, but also staying true to one's roots.

In addition to his family, Matt's early exposure to theater and the arts was instrumental in shaping his future. He grew up in a time when local theater was an integral part of many communities, and Webster Groves was no exception. With a rich local arts scene, Matt found a supportive and inspiring environment in which to nurture his creativity. He became involved in community theater productions, and it was here that he began to take his first steps toward the dream that would eventually lead him to New York and beyond.

Despite being surrounded by a nurturing environment, Matt faced his own share of personal challenges. Like many young people, he struggled with finding his identity in a world that often places value on external appearances. As he navigated adolescence, Matt was not always confident in his own skin. He later revealed that his teenage years were marked by a sense of self-doubt and a longing for validation, a theme he would revisit throughout his life. But it was through acting that Matt found his outlet. The stage became his sanctuary, a place where he could express himself and escape the pressures of adolescence.

It was also during this time that Matt's family instilled in him a sense of perseverance. Despite the inevitable obstacles that came with pursuing a career in acting especially for someone from a small town, Matt was determined to make his dream a reality. He had the support of his family, but more importantly, he had the inner drive to overcome any challenges in his way. His time spent working in community theater solidified his love for performance and made it clear that this was more than just a passing interest, it was his calling.

By the time Matt graduated from high school, he was fully committed to pursuing acting as a career. He moved to New York City to attend "Yale University", where he earned a degree in Theater Arts. Yale's prestigious drama program offered Matt the perfect opportunity to hone his craft and prepare for the professional world of acting. In college, he was able to immerse himself in the study of acting, learning from seasoned professors and peers who shared his passion.

While at Yale, Matt's performances in various college productions earned him the attention of theater professionals. It was here that he gained the confidence and experience needed to enter the competitive world of acting. But despite his talent and drive, New York proved to be a tough city for an aspiring actor. The road to success was never easy, and Matt faced numerous auditions, rejections, and struggles to make a name for himself in the industry. However, he was never deterred. The perseverance he learned in his hometown of Webster Groves continued to serve him well, and with each audition, he became more determined to succeed.

It was during his time in New York that Matt began to land small roles in theater productions and TV shows. His first professional job was a role in the soap opera "Guiding Light", where he portrayed Ben Reade. This was Matt's big break, his first significant acting job and it would serve as the stepping stone that eventually led him to Hollywood. Though his time on "Guiding Light" was relatively brief, it was crucial in building his confidence and reputation as an actor. The exposure he gained from the soap opera led to greater opportunities in both television and film.

Matt's early years in New York were filled with moments of doubt and uncertainty, but they were also the foundation upon which his Hollywood dreams would be built. His commitment to acting, his unwavering work ethic, and the lessons he learned along the way would eventually pay off as he began landing more prominent roles in the years to come.

The early life of Matt Bomer is not just a story of struggle; it is a story of determination, perseverance, and the relentless pursuit of a dream. From his small-town roots in Webster Groves to his transformative years in New York, Matt never wavered from his goal of becoming a successful actor. It was his work ethic, combined with the early support he received from his family and community, that made him the man he is today, someone who would go on to become a household name in Hollywood.

Matt's journey from Webster Groves to New York, and eventually to Los Angeles, is a story of unwavering belief in oneself. The road was never easy, but it was always worth it. As he moved through the ups and downs of his career, Matt held onto the lessons he had learned as a young man: lessons about the importance of hard work, humility, and, above all, staying true to oneself.

CHAPTER TWO

THE ROAD TO FAME – STRUGGLES AND BREAKTHROUGHS

After leaving the comfort of his small-town life in Webster Groves, Matt Bomer arrived in New York City with a singular goal: to become an actor. But the journey to fame was anything but simple. Like many aspiring actors before him, Matt quickly discovered that New York wasn't just a city of opportunities; it was also a city full of rejection, competition, and uncertainty. For someone coming from a small community with little industry experience, the challenges were overwhelming. Yet, Matt faced them with the same determination and drive that had carried him this far.

Upon moving to New York, Matt enrolled at Yale University, joining one of the nation's top drama programs. The prestigious education was a crucial step in his development, allowing him to refine his craft and learn from some of the best instructors in the field. But while Yale provided the tools, it also made Matt realize that success in New York's theater world was no easy feat. The city's theater scene was teeming with talent, and breaking through was a long shot. It was a stark contrast to the small-town stage where Matt had first discovered his passion for acting. No longer was he the standout performer in local productions now, he was one of many, all competing for the same roles and attention.

Despite his impressive academic background and raw talent, Matt found himself facing the typical hurdles that most actors experience when they first arrive in New York: long hours of auditions, rejection after rejection, and a growing sense of doubt. The city, while vibrant and full of opportunity, had a way of wearing down even the most determined. It was a humbling experience. For every callback, there were ten rejections. For every audition, there were more failures than successes. And yet, Matt didn't falter. He knew that breaking into the industry wasn't about instant success—it was about persistence. He kept working, kept auditioning, and kept honing his skills. His passion for acting kept him focused, even during the darkest moments when it seemed like his dream might not come true.

The first significant break in Matt's career came when he landed a role in the long-running soap opera "Guiding Light". His character, Ben Reade, wasn't a lead role, but it was a breakthrough nonetheless. For an actor just starting to make his mark, being cast in a soap opera was a big deal. It wasn't the glitz and glamour of Hollywood, but it was an opportunity, a chance to showcase his abilities to a wide audience. The soap opera world, though often overlooked by mainstream Hollywood, provided valuable exposure and allowed Matt to begin building his resume.

Working on "Guiding Light" was a pivotal moment for Matt. It wasn't just the visibility the role provided that made it so significant—it was the experience itself. Soap operas are known for their fast-paced production schedules, requiring actors to memorize extensive amounts of dialogue in a short period of time. For Matt, this role taught him how to think on his feet and sharpen his skills in a high-pressure environment. It was here that he learned the art of consistency, the importance of bringing something new to each performance, and how to deliver powerful, emotional scenes despite the quick turnaround time. While the role was brief, it provided Matt with the first taste of what it meant to be a professional actor in a highly competitive environment.

However, his time on "Guiding Light" didn't last long, and soon Matt found himself back in the trenches, auditioning for more television and film roles. This period of his career was marked by a series of smaller, often forgettable parts. He appeared in guest spots on television shows like "Chuck" and "Supernatural" and took on minor roles in films that didn't make much of a splash. For many actors, these kinds of roles can be discouraging—small parts that offer little room for growth and don't get the kind of attention that leads to bigger opportunities. But for Matt, these roles were stepping stones, building blocks that allowed him to grow as an actor. He never looked at these parts as failures. Instead, he saw them as a way to refine his craft, learn new things, and gain experience on sets of various sizes and productions.

In the midst of these smaller roles, Matt had to find ways to stay motivated. The entertainment industry is full of rejection, and the road to stardom often feels long and uncertain. But Matt found strength in his unwavering belief that he had something special to offer. He refused to be defined by the small roles he was playing at the time. He was determined to take on projects that challenged him and allowed him to show his range. And that determination eventually paid off.

The breakthrough role that would define Matt Bomer's career came with "Magic Mike", the 2012 film directed by Steven Soderbergh. Playing the role of the smooth and charming male stripper, Matt's performance was nothing short of transformative. While "Magic Mike" was a film that focused on the lives of male exotic dancers, it wasn't just about the choreography or the flashy dance numbers—it was about the characters, their struggles, and their personalities. Matt's role was key in elevating the film, showing audiences that he was more than just a pretty face. He was an actor with depth, someone who could bring authenticity to a character, no matter how unconventional.

The success of "Magic Mike" was monumental for Matt. The film was not only a commercial success, grossing over $167 million worldwide, but it also introduced Matt to a much broader audience. No longer was he a relatively unknown actor doing guest spots on television; he was a star, a leading man in Hollywood. The role in "Magic Mike" changed the trajectory of his career, and with it came new opportunities. Suddenly, Matt was being considered for leading roles in films, and his name became more recognizable to both audiences and industry professionals alike.

But as much as "Magic Mike" helped Matt's career, it also presented challenges. The film's success brought a certain level of expectation, and with that came the pressure to maintain a successful career in Hollywood. The entertainment industry can be unforgiving, and the path from breakout success to sustained fame is often tricky. Yet, Matt handled the pressure with grace. Rather than getting lost in the whirlwind of fame and media attention, he focused on his craft. He took on roles that allowed him to grow as an actor, choosing projects that were challenging and varied. His next major project, "The Normal Heart", saw him take on a complex, emotionally charged role that showcased his ability to handle serious material. This performance earned him critical acclaim and an Emmy nomination, a further testament to his acting chops and versatility.

From "Magic Mike" to "The Normal Heart" to "Fellow Travelers", Matt's career continued to rise as he embraced roles that were both compelling and varied. His journey from New York's theater scene to Hollywood's biggest stages was filled with struggles and breakthroughs, but through it all, Matt remained focused on what mattered most: his passion for acting. The pivotal moments that led to his rise in Hollywood were not without challenges, but they were the result of his hard work, perseverance, and commitment to his craft.

CHAPTER THREE

MAGIC MIKE AND THE TRANSFORMATION

By 2012, Matt Bomer had already made a name for himself in the industry, thanks to his roles in "Guiding Light", "Chuck", and "Supernatural", but he had yet to experience the breakout moment that would define his career. That moment came with "Magic Mike", a film that not only transformed his professional life but also reshaped his public image. While it was a role that seemed to be about physicality and flash, it was Matt's deeper understanding of his character that made his portrayal stand out, offering a unique layer to the movie's otherwise straightforward concept of male strippers.

The casting of Matt Bomer in "Magic Mike" wasn't just a fluke. It was a conscious decision by director Steven Soderbergh, who recognized Matt's potential to bring more than just good looks to the role of "Ken." At the time, Matt had already been building a career based on his charm, good looks, and impressive acting chops. But "Magic Mike" provided him with a platform to show a different side of himself, one that combined humor, vulnerability, and authenticity. While the film's plot focused on the lives of male exotic dancers, the characters were more than just caricatures. Matt's role as Ken, a more sophisticated and reserved dancer, was crucial in balancing the film's tone, adding a layer of subtlety to a genre that many people associated with spectacle rather than depth.

When the film was released, its success was immediate. It became a box office hit, grossing over $167 million worldwide. More than that, "Magic Mike" helped redefine the summer blockbuster by embracing themes of masculinity, desire, and identity. For Matt, the success of the film was transformative. Not only did it open doors for him to take on more prominent roles, but it also positioned him as a leading man in Hollywood, in a way that was both surprising and validating. The film's success confirmed what many in the industry had already suspected that Matt Bomer wasn't just a pretty face; he was a talented actor capable of carrying a major motion picture.

But the role was not without its challenges. As the film grew in popularity, Matt found himself balancing the expectations of his newfound fame with the personal boundaries he had always set for himself. For years, he had kept a relatively low profile, choosing roles that aligned with his values and avoiding the type of fame that might compromise his privacy. But with "Magic Mike" came a whole new level of attention, one that Matt wasn't necessarily prepared for. The public perception of him shifted, he was no longer just the thoughtful, reserved actor known for his television roles. He had become a sex symbol, a status that carried its own set of expectations. Fans, the media, and even industry professionals began to see him as a leading man in a completely different light, one based not only on his acting talent but also on his looks and physical presence.

While many actors would embrace this kind of fame, Matt was cautious. He had always been a private person, and the sudden spotlight brought a level of scrutiny that he had not anticipated. Suddenly, every aspect of his life was open for public consumption, and he had to navigate a new world where his personal boundaries were constantly tested. For someone who had always been more focused on the craft of acting than the celebrity that came with it, the attention was overwhelming at times. But Matt handled the pressure with grace. He continued to take on roles that challenged him and allowed him to grow as an actor, refusing to be defined by his appearance or the roles that had made him famous.

The rise in public attention also brought with it a more complex relationship with fame. While "Magic Mike" was a film that celebrated men's physicality and charisma, it also sparked conversations about gender, sexuality, and societal expectations. Matt's portrayal of Ken was a departure from the stereotypical roles he had played before. It was a subtle yet powerful performance, one that highlighted his ability to portray both the surface and deeper complexities of a character. This role marked a turning point not only for Matt's career but also for how Hollywood viewed him. His ability to step out of the traditional mold and portray a character with both vulnerability and strength helped him carve a unique niche in the industry. It also demonstrated to the world that Matt Bomer was more than just an actor, he was a performer willing to take risks and challenge societal norms.

As Matt's fame skyrocketed, new opportunities quickly followed. Hollywood, recognizing his talent and versatility, began offering him roles in major projects that ranged from action films to dramatic roles. Matt became sought after by top-tier directors and producers, eager to cast him in leading roles. One such project was "The Normal Heart", a film directed by Ryan Murphy, where Matt took on the role of Felix Turner, a character who is grappling with the AIDS crisis in the early days of the epidemic. The film was a massive critical success, and Matt's performance earned him an Emmy nomination for Outstanding Supporting Actor. This role was significant not just for the accolades but for the opportunity it gave Matt to showcase his range as an actor moving away from the more superficial roles he had played in "Magic Mike" to something deeper, more emotional, and historically significant.

The success of "Magic Mike" and the opportunities that followed were pivotal in solidifying Matt's place in Hollywood. However, the transition from a leading man in a summer blockbuster to a respected actor in serious films wasn't easy. The pressure to continue proving himself weighed on him, but he continued to rise to the challenge, taking on roles that allowed him to grow both as an actor and as an individual. As his career advanced, Matt found himself not only starring in films but also becoming a voice for the LGBTQ+ community, using his platform to speak out on issues of equality, representation, and mental health.

In many ways, "Magic Mike" was a double-edged sword for Matt Bomer. It catapulted him into the public eye, offering him opportunities he might not have had otherwise, but it also presented a new set of challenges. The movie gave him a platform to reach millions of fans, but it also forced him to reckon with his newfound status and the demands of fame. Through it all, Matt remained focused on his craft, refusing to be distracted by the trappings of celebrity. Instead, he used his platform to advocate for the causes he believed in and to continue pushing the boundaries of what was possible in his acting career.

The impact of "Magic Mike" on Matt Bomer's career cannot be overstated. It marked a new era for the actor, one where he would no longer be relegated to small roles or television appearances. Instead, he became a leading man in Hollywood, sought after for his talent, his depth, and his ability to portray complex characters. "Magic Mike" didn't just change Matt's career, it transformed him into an icon, redefining how the public saw him and how he saw himself in the industry.

CHAPTER FOUR

FELLOW TRAVELERS AND THE NEW HORIZONS OF HIS CAREER

After a string of breakout roles in "Magic Mike" and "The Normal Heart", Matt Bomer found himself at a crossroads in his career. He had already proven his talent in major Hollywood films, but the question remained: what kind of actor did he want to become? Hollywood had seen Matt's charm, his physical presence, and his ability to portray complex emotions. But in his next major project, "Fellow Travelers", Matt was given the opportunity to showcase a different, deeper layer of his craft. The role would become a defining moment in his career, solidifying his versatility as an actor and his willingness to take on more challenging and nuanced characters.

"Fellow Travelers" is a limited series set in the 1950s, a time when LGBTQ+ individuals faced harsh discrimination and the specter of societal rejection. The show is centered around a forbidden romance between Matt's character, Hawkins Fuller, a State Department official, and Timothy, a younger man played by Jonathan Bailey. The series explores themes of love, political intrigue, betrayal, and the struggle for acceptance during a time of political and social upheaval. It's a role that required Matt to dig deep into the emotional core of a man struggling with his identity in a world that sought to suppress it.

Matt's portrayal of Hawkins Fuller in "Fellow Travelers" is a testament to his acting range. Fuller is a man caught between his public persona and his private life. He is charming, intelligent, and ambitious, but beneath that facade lies a person who is struggling with the burden of keeping his sexuality a secret. The complexity of the character was unlike anything Matt had portrayed before. He had played charming and confident characters, but Fuller was a man torn between two worlds, a man who had to hide a significant part of his identity in order to maintain his position and his sense of self-preservation. In this role, Matt was tasked with showing the pain of a man who longs for love but is forced to deny it in the face of societal pressures.

The significance of this role cannot be overstated. For Matt, playing a character like Hawkins Fuller was not just an opportunity to explore a new side of his acting skills; it was a way to bring attention to a historically marginalized community. The series allowed him to step into the shoes of a man who was not only living in a time of discrimination but was also part of a love story that defied societal norms. In many ways, this was a more personal role for Matt, one that touched on themes of identity, love, and the courage required to live authentically, even in the face of danger.

As the series progressed, viewers watched Matt's character evolve. Hawkins Fuller was initially seen as a man in control, but as his relationship with Timothy deepens, his character begins to unravel. The public and private spheres of his life collide, leading to a series of personal and professional compromises that ultimately push him to the brink. Matt's portrayal of this internal conflict was powerful, showing that the real struggle for Hawkins was not just about navigating the political landscape of the 1950s, it was about reconciling his true self with the person he had to present to the world. Through Matt's performance, Hawkins became a character audiences could empathize with, despite his flaws and imperfections. It was a far cry from the roles that had made him famous, showing the actor's range and proving that he could take on complex, layered characters that demanded more than just surface-level charm.

What made Matt's work on "Fellow Travelers" so impactful was his ability to balance the vulnerability of his character with the strength required to navigate his world. Hawkins Fuller was not a hero in the traditional sense. He was a man caught in a time and place that forced him to hide who he truly was, all while trying to maintain a sense of purpose in his work and in his relationships. Matt's portrayal of this inner turmoil resonated with viewers, adding depth to a character that could have easily been one-dimensional in less capable hands. His performance demonstrated not only his skill as an actor but also his commitment to telling authentic, meaningful stories that had real-world implications.

The success of "Fellow Travelers" further solidified Matt's status as an actor who wasn't content with simply playing safe roles. By choosing this project, he made it clear that he was ready to take on more complex, challenging roles that reflected a broader spectrum of human experiences. His decision to take on "Fellow Travelers" marked a shift in his career, no longer was he just a leading man in romantic comedies or action films. He was now an actor willing to tackle difficult subject matter and portray characters who were multidimensional, even if that meant stepping away from the more conventional roles that had initially brought him fame.

This role also signified Matt's dedication to exploring themes that were important to him personally. Throughout his career, he has been open about his support for LGBTQ+ rights, and "Fellow Travelers" allowed him to put that commitment into action, portraying a character whose struggles with identity mirrored the real-life struggles many LGBTQ+ individuals faced during the mid-20th century. By taking on this role, Matt used his platform to shine a light on the importance of representation and inclusivity, something he has become more vocal about as his career has progressed.

The impact of playing such a layered character extended beyond the screen. "Fellow Travelers" became a critical success, with Matt receiving praise for his portrayal of Hawkins Fuller. The series not only introduced him to a new audience but also reaffirmed his place in Hollywood as a versatile actor capable of tackling a range of roles. His performance was celebrated for its emotional depth and sensitivity, and many critics praised Matt for bringing authenticity to a character that could have easily been lost in the historical context. For Matt, this was not just a career milestone, it was a personal victory, as it allowed him to use his art to make a difference in the lives of others.

As his career continued to evolve, Matt's decision to take on more challenging and diverse roles became a defining characteristic of his acting style. He was no longer just the charming, handsome actor that fans had come to love in "Magic Mike". He was now an actor who took risks, choosing roles that pushed him and challenged his perceptions of what he could accomplish. From his portrayal of a man caught in a forbidden love affair in "Fellow Travelers" to more dramatic roles in "The Boys in the Band" and beyond, Matt's acting journey continued to surprise and inspire. Each new project showed his ability to evolve as an actor, and it was clear that he was more than just a leading man, he was a serious artist, committed to telling stories that mattered.

Through his work on "Fellow Travelers" and other recent projects, Matt Bomer has proven that he is an actor who is not afraid to take risks, push boundaries, and bring complex characters to life. His ability to navigate the emotional and psychological depth of his roles has solidified his place as one of Hollywood's most respected actors. What started as a career filled with glamorous roles has transformed into a career of substance, one that reflects Matt's growth not only as an actor but as an individual.

The impact of "Fellow Travelers" Matt's career cannot be overstated. It was a role that marked the next phase of his professional life, showing that he was more than just a pretty face in a summer blockbuster. It was a role that proved Matt Bomer's versatility and commitment to his craft, and it will remain one of the standout achievements in his already impressive career.

CHAPTER FIVE

AWARDS AND RECOGNITION – THE CRITICAL ACCLAIM

As Matt Bomer's career continued to soar, it was clear that his talent was not going unnoticed. From his early days in soap operas to his breakout roles in feature films, it was evident that he was not just another handsome face in Hollywood, he was a true actor, capable of delivering powerful and nuanced performances. But it wasn't until he took on the role of Felix Turner in "The Normal Heart" that Matt's work began to receive the kind of critical acclaim that would change the trajectory of his career and solidify his place as one of Hollywood's most respected actors.

In 2014, Matt was cast in the film adaptation of "The Normal Heart", a powerful drama directed by Ryan Murphy. Based on the Tony Award-winning play by Larry Kramer, the film centers around the early years of the AIDS epidemic in New York City during the 1980s. Matt's portrayal of Felix Turner, a reporter diagnosed with AIDS, was a career-defining moment. His performance was both heartbreaking and deeply human, capturing the emotional complexity of a man who is facing an unimaginable crisis while trying to hold onto love, hope, and dignity.

"The Normal Heart" was a critical success, receiving numerous accolades, and Matt's performance was one of the standout elements of the film. His portrayal of Felix earned him an "Emmy nomination" for Outstanding Supporting Actor in a Limited Series or Television Movie. For Matt, this recognition was not just a validation of his talent, but a reminder that his hard work, dedication, and emotional depth had not gone unnoticed. The role gave Matt a platform to showcase his range as an actor, moving beyond the charming roles he was known for and into more dramatic, weighty material. It was a breakthrough moment in his career, and one that marked a turning point, Matt was now being recognized as a serious actor, capable of handling complex, emotionally charged roles.

The "Emmy nomination" was a significant milestone for Matt, but it was just the beginning of the recognition he would receive in the years that followed. The success of "The Normal Heart" led to even greater opportunities, and Matt continued to take on roles that challenged him and pushed him to grow as an actor. Whether it was in films like "The Magnificent Seven" or the "Fellow Travelers" series, Matt's performances continued to receive praise from critics and audiences alike. But it wasn't just the critics who took notice, Matt was also earning the respect of his peers in the industry.

In 2018, Matt's career reached new heights when he won a "Golden Globe" for his role in "The Normal Heart". Winning the award was a moment of immense pride for Matt, as it not only recognized his talent but also the importance of the story he had helped bring to life. The Golden Globe was a testament to Matt's skill as an actor, but it was also a nod to the significance of the film itself—an exploration of a pivotal moment in history and a reminder of the lives lost to AIDS during the early years of the epidemic.

For Matt, winning a Golden Globe was both humbling and empowering. It wasn't just about the trophy or the recognition, it was about the impact of the story and the fact that he had been part of something much bigger than himself. The win solidified Matt's place in Hollywood as one of the industry's most talented and respected actors. It was a moment that would mark his career for years to come, and it signaled a shift in how Matt was perceived in the industry. No longer was he just the charming actor with a great smile, he was now a Golden Globe-winning actor who had proven his versatility and depth.

But despite the accolades and recognition, Matt has always remained grounded. He is often quick to deflect the praise he receives, preferring to focus on the work rather than the awards. In interviews, he's made it clear that for him, the real reward is not the trophy, it's the opportunity to be a part of meaningful stories and to create art that resonates with people. For Matt, the recognition is a byproduct of his passion for the craft of acting. He is driven not by fame or accolades but by the desire to tell stories that matter, to portray characters that are real, relatable, and emotionally complex.

This humility and perspective on success have made Matt a respected figure in Hollywood, not just for his talent but for his character. He has built a reputation as someone who is dedicated to his work, respectful of the craft, and humble in the face of success. Industry professionals admire his commitment to his roles, his professionalism on set, and his willingness to take on challenging material. Matt is known for his meticulous approach to his work, spending hours studying the characters he plays and ensuring that each performance is authentic and true to the story.

In addition to his acting talent, Matt has also become a role model for many in the industry, particularly for young actors and members of the LGBTQ+ community. He has been open about his journey as a gay man in Hollywood, and he has used his platform to advocate for greater representation and inclusivity. Matt has shown that it's possible to be both true to yourself and successful in an industry that often demands conformity. His success is a reminder that talent, dedication, and authenticity are what truly matter in the world of entertainment, and it's these qualities that have earned him the admiration of his peers and fans alike.

As Matt continues to rise in Hollywood, his career serves as a blueprint for aspiring actors showing that success isn't just about the roles you take, but about the dedication, perseverance, and heart you bring to your work. His journey from television guest spots to being a Golden Globe-winning actor is a testament to the power of staying true to your vision and believing in your own potential, even when the odds are stacked against you. Through it all, Matt has maintained his integrity, remained grounded, and continued to push boundaries as an actor, choosing roles that challenge him and allow him to grow.

As he looks to the future, Matt Bomer's place in Hollywood is secure. He has earned his recognition through hard work, dedication, and a commitment to excellence. But for Matt, the journey isn't over. With each new project, he continues to evolve as an artist, taking on roles that challenge him and allow him to explore new dimensions of his craft. His story is far from finished, there is still so much more to come from this talented and driven actor.

CHAPTER SIX

PERSONAL LIFE – THE MAN BEHIND THE ACTOR

Behind the glitz and glamour of Hollywood, Matt Bomer has always remained remarkably private. Known for his reserved nature, the actor has always managed to keep his personal life separate from his public persona. While his career has taken him to the highest echelons of the entertainment industry, Matt has stayed grounded, focusing on his family, his relationships, and the values that have guided him since his early days in Missouri.

Growing up in Webster Groves, Missouri, Matt was raised in a family that valued education, hard work, and personal integrity. His parents, while not involved in the entertainment industry, instilled in him the importance of staying true to oneself and working toward one's dreams. This upbringing would later shape how Matt approached both his career and personal life. His parents' support for his passion for acting gave him the confidence to pursue his dreams, but they also taught him to remain humble and to always prioritize his values above fame or success.

From a young age, Matt demonstrated a strong sense of self-awareness, something that would become essential as he navigated the complexities of fame and personal identity in Hollywood. While many public figures are known for their extroverted personalities and constant public presence, Matt has always maintained a quieter, more introspective approach to life. This has allowed him to maintain a sense of normalcy, even as his career has skyrocketed.

A pivotal moment in Matt's personal life came in 2012, when he made the decision to publicly come out as gay. At the time, the entertainment industry was still grappling with the challenges of LGBTQ+ visibility, especially in mainstream Hollywood. Coming out wasn't just a personal decision for Matt, it was a statement. He knew that by sharing this part of his life with the public, he could potentially face backlash, and yet he felt it was important to live authentically. In a world where many actors, particularly those in the early years of their careers, hid their sexuality for fear of being typecast or losing opportunities, Matt took a bold step forward. His decision was not just about his own personal truth, but also about sending a message of visibility and acceptance to others who might be struggling with their own identities.

The impact of Matt's decision to come out publicly was significant, both personally and professionally. On a personal level, Matt found immense freedom in being able to live openly, without the weight of hiding his true self. For years, he had balanced his public persona with the need for privacy, but coming out allowed him to embrace a part of his life that had previously been kept behind closed doors. It was a cathartic experience, one that brought him closer to himself and to the people who mattered most.

Professionally, the reaction to Matt's coming out was overwhelmingly positive. While there were some critics, the majority of his fans and colleagues supported him wholeheartedly. His career continued to thrive, and in many ways, coming out strengthened his position as an actor. Rather than being pigeonholed into one specific type of role, Matt became known not just for his talent, but also for his authenticity. His decision to embrace his identity helped pave the way for more LGBTQ+ actors to feel comfortable doing the same, creating a ripple effect that continues to be felt in Hollywood today.

One of the most important aspects of Matt's personal life is his relationship with his husband, Simon Halls. The couple married in 2011, and they have since built a life together, away from the public eye. Simon Halls, a Hollywood public relations executive, has been a steadfast partner for Matt throughout his career. Together, they've created a family that remains largely private, away from the prying eyes of the media. Their commitment to each other, as well as to their children, has been a cornerstone of Matt's personal life.

While many Hollywood couples are often thrust into the spotlight, Matt and Simon have managed to maintain a strong, supportive relationship without becoming a tabloid fixture. They have three children together, and Matt has often spoken about how important his family is to him. Despite the demands of his career, Matt prioritizes his family life, ensuring that his children grow up in a stable, loving environment. This commitment to his family, coupled with his desire for privacy, has allowed Matt to maintain a sense of normalcy in an industry that often thrives on drama and spectacle.

The importance of privacy is something Matt has emphasized throughout his career. While many actors are eager to share every aspect of their personal lives with the public, Matt has always maintained a careful balance between his professional and personal worlds. For him, keeping a sense of privacy has been crucial in preserving his mental well-being and ensuring that his family remains safe from the intrusive nature of celebrity culture. In a society that often elevates celebrities to an almost god-like status, Matt's desire for normalcy serves as a reminder that actors are human too, and they deserve the same privacy and respect as anyone else.

In interviews, Matt has spoken about how his personal life influences his work as an actor. He believes that his relationships, particularly his marriage and family life, have made him a better actor. The love and support he receives from Simon and their children have helped him navigate the challenges of fame and the often demanding nature of Hollywood. It has also given him a deeper understanding of the emotional complexities of the characters he plays. As an actor, Matt is known for his ability to bring depth and vulnerability to his roles, and much of that comes from the emotional experiences he's had in his own life.

Despite the public nature of his career, Matt has always made a concerted effort to shield his loved ones from the limelight. He's not one to post personal details on social media or share every moment of his family life with the world. Instead, he has chosen to keep his personal world private, focusing on the work that matters most—his family and his acting. In an age where social media often dictates the narrative of a celebrity's life, Matt's decision to remain private has set him apart from many of his peers.

His ability to separate his public and private lives has allowed him to maintain his authenticity and remain true to his core values. Matt has never been one to chase fame for the sake of fame; his passion for acting has always been about the craft and the opportunity to tell meaningful stories. As he continues to rise in Hollywood, his focus remains on his work, his family, and the things that truly matter to him.

In many ways, Matt Bomer's personal life has been a grounding force throughout his career. His decision to live authentically, his commitment to his family, and his belief in the importance of privacy have shaped the way he navigates Hollywood. While his career continues to evolve and grow, he remains true to the values that were instilled in him from a young age: hard work, humility, and the importance of being true to oneself.

CHAPTER SEVEN

ADVOCACY AND PHILANTHROPY – GIVING BACK TO THE COMMUNITY

While Matt Bomer's career is defined by his talent, versatility, and dedication to the craft of acting, his impact extends far beyond the silver screen. Known for his commitment to authenticity and integrity, Matt has used his platform to support causes that matter deeply to him. One of the most notable aspects of his life has been his work with charitable organizations and his advocacy for the LGBTQ+ community. Matt's journey in Hollywood has been marked by a desire to not only be recognized for his acting but to also make a tangible difference in the world.

From his earliest years in the public eye, Matt has been open about his identity as a gay man. His decision to come out publicly in 2012 was a significant moment not just for him personally, but for the wider LGBTQ+ community. At a time when visibility was still a major challenge for many LGBTQ+ actors in

Hollywood, Matt's decision to embrace his true self was a beacon of hope for others. He became a symbol of the possibility of success without hiding one's identity, and that authenticity is something he has carried with him throughout his career.

In the years following his coming out, Matt has used his voice to advocate for LGBTQ+ rights and raise awareness about the issues that still affect the community. He has been a vocal supporter of same-sex marriage, and he has consistently worked to challenge stereotypes and promote inclusivity within Hollywood. For Matt, the fight for LGBTQ+ rights is not just about being a public figure, it's about making real, lasting change. He has partnered with various organizations, including the "GLAAD" organization, which works to accelerate LGBTQ+ acceptance, and the "Human Rights Campaign", one of the country's largest LGBTQ+ civil rights organizations.

Beyond advocating for the LGBTQ+ community, Matt has become a passionate supporter of mental health awareness. In an industry where mental health can often be an afterthought, Matt has been outspoken about his own experiences and the importance of maintaining emotional well-being. He has spoken candidly in interviews about the pressures of fame and the toll it can take on one's mental health. His openness has encouraged others to seek help and to destigmatize mental health issues. Matt has also worked with organizations like "The Trevor Project", a leading national organization providing crisis intervention and suicide prevention services to LGBTQ+ young people. Through his partnership with these organizations, Matt has helped raise awareness about the mental health struggles that many LGBTQ+ individuals face, especially young people who are still coming to terms with their identities in a sometimes hostile world.

In addition to mental health, Matt has been a longtime advocate for "AIDS awareness". His role in "The Normal Heart" was a significant part of his journey into activism, as it brought to the forefront the ongoing HIV/AIDS epidemic, particularly its impact on the gay community. Through his work with organizations like "AIDS Project Los Angeles" and the "Elizabeth Glaser Pediatric AIDS Foundation", Matt has been instrumental in raising awareness about the continuing fight against HIV/AIDS and the need for both research and support for those living with the virus. The film "The Normal Heart" gave him the opportunity to portray the deeply emotional story of Felix Turner, a character living with AIDS in the early years of the epidemic, which struck a personal chord with Matt. His portrayal of Felix was not just a role, it was a chance to honor the many lives lost to the disease and to draw attention to the ongoing work that still needs to be done in the fight against HIV/AIDS.

Through his philanthropic efforts, Matt has come to understand the profound satisfaction that comes from giving back to the community. For him, using his platform for activism isn't just about advocacy, it's about leaving a lasting, positive impact. His experiences have shown him that true fulfillment comes not just from professional success, but from contributing to something greater than oneself. He often speaks about the importance of using one's position of privilege to make a difference, particularly for those who may not have the same platform or access to resources. As a public figure, Matt recognizes that he has the ability to draw attention to causes that need support, and he takes that responsibility seriously.

Despite his many charitable endeavors, Matt is humble about his role in these movements. He does not seek attention or praise for his activism. Instead, he believes that the work speaks for itself. His commitment to these causes has always been driven by a genuine desire to help others, not by the pursuit of accolades or recognition. Matt has expressed how meaningful it is to see the change that can come from collective action, and how fulfilling it is to know that his efforts, even in small ways, can make a difference in someone's life.

Matt's personal satisfaction in giving back is also reflected in his relationship with his family. He has often mentioned how much his family's support has meant to him throughout his career, and how they have encouraged him to stay focused on the things that matter most. His work with charitable organizations and his dedication to causes close to his heart are not just career choices, they are integral to his identity. For Matt, success in Hollywood means little if it doesn't also come with the opportunity to give back and make a meaningful contribution to the world.

Matt has also found fulfillment in his role as a father and husband, recognizing that family life provides him with the grounding and stability he needs to continue his work in the entertainment industry and in activism. His relationship with Simon Halls, whom he married in 2011, and their three children have provided him with a source of love and support that anchors him in an industry that can often feel chaotic and transient. He has spoken openly about how his family has helped him maintain a sense of balance and perspective, allowing him to continue pursuing his passions with a sense of purpose beyond the career spotlight.

Through his advocacy, Matt Bomer has proven that fame can be used for far more than self-promotion, it can be used to promote change, create awareness, and positively impact society. His involvement in causes related to the LGBTQ+ community, mental health, and AIDS awareness has left an indelible mark on the entertainment industry and beyond. For Matt, advocacy isn't a side project; it's a core part of who he is. It reflects his values, his commitment to justice, and his belief that everyone, regardless of background or identity, deserves to be seen, heard, and treated with dignity.

As Matt continues to thrive in his acting career, his advocacy work serves as a reminder of the power of using one's voice for good. In an industry where the spotlight can often overshadow the real work that needs to be done, Matt Bomer stands as an example of an actor who is not just content to take on roles for fame or fortune. Instead, he has used his success to further important causes and to create a better world for future generations. His commitment to advocacy and philanthropy continues to inspire those who look up to him, not just as an actor, but as a role model who has used his platform to make the world a better place.

CHAPTER EIGHT

NAVIGATING THE FAME – BALANCING HOLLYWOOD'S DEMANDS WITH PERSONAL VALUES

The world of Hollywood can be a thrilling, yet daunting, place. It is a realm where fame and success come at the cost of one's privacy and freedom. For Matt Bomer, navigating this demanding and often chaotic industry has been an ongoing challenge, one that he has met with remarkable poise, discipline, and self-awareness. From his early days as an aspiring actor in New York to becoming a household name in Hollywood, Matt has always sought to maintain a sense of balance and authenticity, even as the spotlight grew brighter.

The realities of fame are not always as glamorous as they seem on the surface. While it brings opportunities and recognition, it also brings its own set of pressures. The constant attention from the media, the expectations of fans, and the ever-present scrutiny from the public can take a toll on an individual. For many, the lure of fame can lead to a loss of personal identity, as they find themselves conforming to the industry's standards of what is expected. But Matt, from the outset, has been determined to avoid falling into that trap. He has always been clear about the importance of maintaining his personal values, no matter how much his career may demand of him.

At the core of Matt's approach to fame is a commitment to authenticity. Unlike many celebrities who feel the need to constantly share their personal lives with the world, Matt has chosen to keep his private life just that private. While he is open about his experiences and values, he does not feel the need to air every detail of his life for public consumption. This has allowed him to keep a clear boundary between his career and personal life, ensuring that his sense of self remains intact even as his public persona expands.

In Hollywood, where the lines between personal and professional can often blur, maintaining this boundary can be difficult. The demands of the industry—press tours, interviews, red carpet events often come with little room for downtime or personal reflection. Yet Matt has consistently shown that it is possible to thrive in Hollywood without losing sight of what truly matters. He has made it a point to focus on the work itself, rather than getting caught up in the superficial aspects of fame. For Matt, it has always been about the craft of acting—creating authentic, meaningful performances that resonate with audiences rather than chasing the fame that often accompanies success in the industry.

A significant aspect of Matt's ability to maintain this balance is his "approach to work-life balance". In an industry where long hours and constant travel are the norm, it is easy for work to take precedence over everything else. Yet, Matt has managed to carve out time for the things that are most important to him—his family, his personal well-being, and his advocacy work. He has been vocal about the challenges of maintaining a healthy balance, but also about how he has made it a priority to preserve his sense of normalcy. In interviews, Matt has often spoken about how important it is to stay grounded and to keep a clear perspective on what really matters. He recognizes that fame is fleeting and that the things that truly provide fulfillment like family and personal growth are the ones worth prioritizing.

For Matt, a key element of this balance is ensuring that he remains true to himself. He knows that being authentic to who he is, both as an actor and as an individual, is essential to maintaining his sense of peace and happiness. It's easy for celebrities to get lost in the hype, to become consumed by the attention and accolades, but Matt has always resisted this temptation. Instead, he remains focused on the work that fulfills him creatively and emotionally, and on staying connected to the people who matter most, his family and close friends.

Another crucial factor in Matt's ability to navigate fame with grace is the "support system" that surrounds him. Matt has been fortunate to have a strong and loving family who has supported him throughout his career, and this has played a significant role in helping him maintain his equilibrium. His husband, Simon Halls, has been a constant presence in his life, providing stability and emotional support in a world that often feels unstable. Simon, a public relations executive, understands the pressures of the industry, and together, they have created a private, grounded family life that is a safe haven from the scrutiny of Hollywood.

Matt often credits his family for helping him stay grounded, especially during the most challenging times of his career. Their unwavering support has given him the strength to remain focused on his values, rather than getting swept up in the whirlwind of fame. It is through his family that Matt has learned the importance of maintaining boundaries, setting priorities, and protecting his personal well-being. This foundation of love and support has allowed Matt to weather the ups and downs of his career, all while maintaining a sense of balance and peace.

Despite the overwhelming pressures of Hollywood, Matt has also made it a point to "prioritize his mental and physical well-being". In an industry that often glorifies overwork and burnout, Matt's approach to maintaining his health has been both refreshing and vital. He believes in the importance of self-care and has spoken publicly about the need to take breaks, spend time with loved ones, and engage in activities that bring joy and relaxation. Whether it's spending time with his children, enjoying outdoor activities, or engaging in creative hobbies outside of acting, Matt understands that maintaining his health is not just about physical fitness, it's about emotional and mental balance, too.

Navigating the fame that comes with Hollywood stardom requires a unique blend of resilience, self-awareness, and a solid foundation of support. For Matt Bomer, the ability to maintain his personal values and sense of normalcy has been the key to balancing the demands of his career with his personal life. By focusing on what truly matters—his family, his health, and his authenticity, Matt has built a life and a career that are rooted in purpose. He is a reminder that success in Hollywood doesn't have to come at the expense of one's integrity or happiness. Through hard work, dedication, and the support of those closest to him, Matt Bomer has shown that it is possible to thrive in the spotlight while remaining true to oneself.

CHAPTER NINE

THE FUTURE – CONTINUING TO EVOLVE AS AN ACTOR AND HUMAN BEING

As Matt Bomer's career continues to soar, one question lingers on the minds of fans and industry professionals alike: what's next for this talented actor? Having already achieved significant milestones in his career, from iconic roles in "Magic Mike" to his Emmy-nominated performance in "The Normal Heart", Matt Bomer shows no signs of slowing down. In fact, as he enters the next phase of his career, he is poised to continue evolving both as an actor and as a human being. With a string of upcoming projects and a renewed focus on producing, Matt is embracing the future with the same dedication and passion that has defined his career thus far.

Matt's "upcoming projects" reveal his continued commitment to diversifying his roles and pushing boundaries as an actor. In 2025, he will star in "Fellow Travelers", a series that promises to showcase his range and depth as an actor. The show, which is based on the critically acclaimed novel by Thomas Mallon, explores the complexities of love, politics, and personal identity against the backdrop of the 1950s and 1960s. This project is particularly important to Matt because it combines historical significance with deeply personal themes of identity and love. Playing a character in a time of such political and social upheaval gives Matt the chance to delve into emotional and complex terrain. For Matt, this isn't just a role; it's an opportunity to tell a powerful story that resonates with his own advocacy work, particularly regarding LGBTQ+ rights and visibility.

In addition to "Fellow Travelers", Matt has several film and television projects lined up. The "diversity of his roles" reflects his desire to keep evolving as an actor, choosing projects that challenge him to grow and expand his range. Whether it's a role in an intense drama, a quirky comedy, or even a role in a superhero film, Matt is committed to taking on roles that excite him and allow him to stretch his abilities. He has expressed his interest in working on more "groundbreaking, thought-provoking material", and his upcoming work suggests he's ready to explore even more complex characters and narratives.

As Matt moves forward in his career, he has also expressed a desire to move into "producing". His passion for storytelling has grown beyond acting, and he sees producing as an opportunity to have more creative control over the projects he's involved in. By stepping into the role of producer, Matt hopes to bring new voices and diverse perspectives to the entertainment industry. He is deeply committed to championing stories that reflect the world's complexity, with an emphasis on representing underrepresented communities, particularly in the LGBTQ+ space. For Matt, being a producer means not only selecting projects that resonate with him personally but also working to create a more inclusive and diverse media landscape.

Matt's "aspirations as an actor and producer" are driven by his desire to make a lasting impact on the entertainment industry. He has already achieved so much as an actor, but for him, the next step is about shaping the future of Hollywood. By becoming more involved in the creative process, Matt seeks to ensure that the stories told reflect the full spectrum of human experience. He is particularly passionate about continuing to advocate for LGBTQ+ representation in film and television. As a gay man in Hollywood, Matt understands the importance of visibility and feels a strong responsibility to be a part of that change. His work as a producer will allow him to take a more active role in this mission, using his influence to open doors for others in the industry and elevate stories that might otherwise go unheard.

One of the things that stands out about Matt's "vision for the future" is his desire to create work that not only entertains but also educates and inspires. He believes that stories can change the world by showing the complexities of human relationships, by giving a voice to the voiceless, and by challenging societal norms. As Matt continues to take on roles that challenge him personally and professionally, he remains committed to making an impact through his work. Whether through acting or producing, Matt's goal is to leave behind a legacy of meaningful storytelling that has a positive, lasting effect on the entertainment industry and its audience.

As Matt looks to the future, he also takes time to reflect on the "evolution of his career and personal growth". When he first started out in Hollywood, Matt was focused on making a name for himself. But over time, he has come to realize that success is not just about fame or accolades. True success, for Matt, lies in doing work that he's passionate about and that speaks to his values. He has always been driven by a sense of purpose using his platform for advocacy, choosing roles that challenge him as an actor, and striving to be a positive influence in Hollywood. Looking back on his career, Matt sees the various roles he's taken on as more than just acting jobs; they are a reflection of his journey as a human being. Each role has allowed him to grow as an artist and as a person, teaching him new lessons about empathy, vulnerability, and strength.

Matt's personal growth has mirrored his professional growth. As he's navigated the highs and lows of fame, he has learned to prioritize what matters most—his family, his values, and his authenticity. He recognizes that the entertainment industry is constantly changing, and that with each new role, he is given the chance to evolve. But no matter how much his career may change, Matt remains committed to staying true to himself. His values—integrity, authenticity, and a commitment to giving back are what have guided him from his early days in New York to his current success in Hollywood.

Looking to the future, Matt sees his career as a journey, not a destination. He's excited for the roles yet to come, the opportunities to grow as an actor and producer, and the chance to continue using his platform for social good. He envisions a Hollywood that is more inclusive, more diverse, and more focused on telling the stories that matter. He wants to be a part of that change, and with his talent, his influence, and his commitment to his values, there's no doubt that he will continue to make an impact in the entertainment industry for years to come.

As Matt Bomer continues to evolve as both an actor and a human being, one thing is clear: the best is yet to come. His dedication to his craft, his commitment to advocating for the underrepresented, and his focus on leaving a meaningful legacy will ensure that his journey is one of continued success and growth. Whether he's portraying complex characters on screen, producing groundbreaking work behind the scenes, or using his voice to make a difference, Matt will undoubtedly remain a force in Hollywood, one whose career continues to inspire, challenge, and elevate those around him.

CONCLUSION

A LEGACY OF PASSION, TALENT, AND AUTHENTICITY

As Matt Bomer's career continues to soar, one question lingers on the minds of fans and industry professionals alike: what's next for this talented actor? Having already achieved significant milestones in his career, from iconic roles in "Magic Mike" to his Emmy-nominated performance in "The Normal Heart", Matt Bomer shows no signs of slowing down. In fact, as he enters the next phase of his career, he is poised to continue evolving both as an actor and as a human being. With a string of upcoming projects and a renewed focus on producing, Matt is embracing the future with the same dedication and passion that has defined his career thus far.

Matt's "upcoming projects" reveal his continued commitment to diversifying his roles and pushing boundaries as an actor. In 2025, he will star in "Fellow Travelers", a series that promises to showcase his range and depth as an actor. The show, which is based on the critically acclaimed novel by Thomas Mallon, explores the complexities of love, politics, and personal identity against the backdrop of the 1950s and 1960s. This project is particularly important to Matt because it combines historical significance with deeply personal themes of identity and love. Playing a character in a time of such political and social upheaval gives Matt the chance to delve into emotional and complex terrain. For Matt, this isn't just a role; it's an opportunity to tell a powerful story that resonates with his own advocacy work, particularly regarding LGBTQ+ rights and visibility.

In addition to "Fellow Travelers", Matt has several film and television projects lined up. The "diversity of his roles" reflects his desire to keep evolving as an actor, choosing projects that challenge him to grow and expand his range. Whether it's a role in an intense drama, a quirky comedy, or even a role in a superhero film, Matt is committed to taking on roles that excite him and allow him to stretch his abilities. He has expressed his interest in working on more "groundbreaking, thought-provoking material", and his upcoming work suggests he's ready to explore even more complex characters and narratives.

As Matt moves forward in his career, he has also expressed a desire to move into "producing". His passion for storytelling has grown beyond acting, and he sees producing as an opportunity to have more creative control over the projects he's involved in. By stepping into the role of producer, Matt hopes to bring new voices and diverse perspectives to the entertainment industry. He is deeply committed to championing stories that reflect the world's complexity, with an emphasis on representing underrepresented communities, particularly in the LGBTQ+ space. For Matt, being a producer means not only selecting projects that resonate with him personally but also working to create a more inclusive and diverse media landscape.

Matt's "aspirations as an actor and producer" are driven by his desire to make a lasting impact on the entertainment industry. He has already achieved so much as an actor, but for him, the next step is about shaping the future of Hollywood. By becoming more involved in the creative process, Matt seeks to ensure that the stories told reflect the full spectrum of human experience. He is particularly passionate about continuing to advocate for LGBTQ+ representation in film and television. As a gay man in Hollywood, Matt understands the importance of visibility and feels a strong responsibility to be a part of that change. His work as a producer will allow him to take a more active role in this mission, using his influence to open doors for others in the industry and elevate stories that might otherwise go unheard.

One of the things that stands out about Matt's "vision for the future" is his desire to create work that not only entertains but also educates and inspires. He believes that stories can change the world by showing the complexities of human relationships, by giving a voice to the voiceless, and by challenging societal norms. As Matt continues to take on roles that challenge him personally and professionally, he remains committed to making an impact through his work. Whether through acting or producing, Matt's goal is to leave behind a legacy of meaningful storytelling that has a positive, lasting effect on the entertainment industry and its audience.

As Matt looks to the future, he also takes time to reflect on the "evolution of his career and personal growth". When he first started out in Hollywood, Matt was focused on making a name for himself. But over time, he has come to realize that success is not just about fame or accolades. True success, for Matt, lies in doing work that he's passionate about and that speaks to his values. He has always been driven by a sense of purpose using his platform for advocacy, choosing roles that challenge him as an actor, and striving to be a positive influence in Hollywood. Looking back on his career, Matt sees the various roles he's taken on as more than just acting jobs; they are a reflection of his journey as a human being. Each role has allowed him to grow as an artist and as a person, teaching him new lessons about empathy, vulnerability, and strength.

Matt's personal growth has mirrored his professional growth. As he's navigated the highs and lows of fame, he has learned to prioritize what matters most—his family, his values, and his authenticity. He recognizes that the entertainment industry is constantly changing, and that with each new role, he is given the chance to evolve. But no matter how much his career may change, Matt remains committed to staying true to himself. His values—integrity, authenticity, and a commitment to giving back are what have guided him from his early days in New York to his current success in Hollywood.

Looking to the future, Matt sees his career as a journey, not a destination. He's excited for the roles yet to come, the opportunities to grow as an actor and producer, and the chance to continue using his platform for social good. He envisions a Hollywood that is more inclusive, more diverse, and more focused on telling the stories that matter. He wants to be a part of that change, and with his talent, his influence, and his commitment to his values, there's no doubt that he will continue to make an impact in the entertainment industry for years to come.

As Matt Bomer continues to evolve as both an actor and a human being, one thing is clear: the best is yet to come. His dedication to his craft, his commitment to advocating for the underrepresented, and his focus on leaving a meaningful legacy will ensure that his journey is one of continued success and growth. Whether he's portraying complex characters on screen, producing groundbreaking work behind the scenes, or using his voice to make a difference, Matt will undoubtedly remain a force in Hollywood, one whose career continues to inspire, challenge, and elevate those around him.

BONUS CHAPTER
FUN FACTS, TRIBUTES, AND MATT'S LEGACY IN POP CULTURE

Matt Bomer's career has been full of memorable roles, stunning performances, and a passion for storytelling that has resonated with fans and industry professionals alike. But beyond the accolades and roles that have defined his career, there are many "fun facts" and lesser-known details about Matt's personal life and journey that paint a more intimate picture of the man behind the iconic characters.

Fun Facts About Matt Bomer

1. **He's a Master of Impersonations**
   While Matt is known for his compelling acting skills, he has an impressive ability to do impersonations. Over the years, he's shown his friends and colleagues that he has quite a talent for mimicking voices and personalities. Whether it's famous actors or comedians, Matt can pull off a spot-on impersonation, often

using this skill for fun on set or during interviews.

2. A Love for Music

Many fans may not know that Matt Bomer has a deep love for music. He was involved in musical theater in college and has even showcased his vocal talents in certain roles. He performed a memorable duet with ""Kristin Chenoweth"" in "The Normal Heart"—a brief but powerful moment that showed off his impressive voice. Music has always been a passion of his, and he has admitted that if he hadn't pursued acting, he might have explored a career in the music industry.

3. He's an Avid Collector

Matt has a love for "antique furniture" and is known for being an avid collector of vintage items. He enjoys finding rare pieces that tell a story and has developed a keen eye for quality craftsmanship. This interest in antiques reflects his appreciation for history, artistry, and timelessness, traits that also shine through in his acting choices.

4. **His Iconic Role in "Chuck" Was Originally Supposed to Be a One-Off**
Matt's role in "Chuck" as the charming and mysterious Bryce Larkin was initially intended to be a "one-off" appearance. However, his charismatic performance and undeniable chemistry with the rest of the cast led to him becoming a recurring character. His role became one of the fan favorites, and it's still a standout moment in his early career.

5. **He's a Family-Oriented Person**
While Matt keeps his personal life relatively private, it is well-known that he is incredibly close to his family. His relationship with his husband, "Simon Halls", and their three children are a cornerstone of his life. He often speaks about how important family is to him and how it keeps him grounded amidst the hustle and bustle of Hollywood. Family is a source of strength for Matt,

and he credits them for helping him stay true to his values and navigate the pressures of fame.

Tributes from Co-Stars, Directors, and Industry Colleagues

Matt Bomer's professionalism, kindness, and dedication to his craft have earned him the respect of his peers in the entertainment industry. Over the years, many of his co-stars, directors, and colleagues have shared their admiration for him, both on and off the set.

Ryan Murphy, the director of "The Normal Heart" and a long-time collaborator, has often spoken about Matt's "dedication" to the craft of acting. "Matt Bomer is one of the finest actors I've ever worked with," Murphy once said. "He brings such depth and authenticity to every role he plays. His performance in "The Normal Heart" was nothing short of extraordinary, and it was one of the most rewarding experiences of my career."

Kristin Chenoweth, who shared a screen with Matt in "The Normal Heart", praised his professionalism and kindness. "Matt is one of those actors who lights up a room, not just with his looks, but with his heart. He's truly a wonderful human being, and his talent is unmatched. Working with him was such an honor."

Simon Halls, Matt's husband, is not only a support system but a fellow advocate for important causes. In interviews, he has spoken about Matt's quiet strength and unwavering commitment to using his platform for good. "Matt is the kind of person who always wants to make a difference. He's incredibly humble and grounded, but he has this tremendous heart and passion for helping others."

Michael Sheen, who starred alongside Matt in "The Normal Heart", echoed similar sentiments, noting how Matt's performance elevated the film. "Matt has this incredible ability to make the audience feel everything his character feels. He doesn't just act, he becomes the character. His performance is raw and real, and that's something special."

Matt Bomer's Legacy in Pop Culture

As Matt Bomer's career has grown, his influence on pop culture has only deepened. From his breakout role in "Magic Mike" to his critical acclaim in "The Normal Heart", Matt's image has become synonymous with versatility, vulnerability, and authenticity. He has carved out a place for himself as a leading man who is not just admired for his looks, but respected for his acting skills and his advocacy for LGBTQ+ rights.

One of the key elements of Matt's legacy is how he has changed the way Hollywood views representation. As a gay actor who has openly embraced his sexuality, Matt has become a role model for many LGBTQ+ individuals, showing that success in Hollywood is possible without hiding who you are. His courage in coming out at a time when many actors chose to keep their sexuality private has inspired countless others to embrace their true selves.

Matt's impact on LGBTQ+ visibility in Hollywood is undeniable, and his work in both film and television continues to challenge norms and redefine what it means to be a leading man.

Matt's legacy also extends to the roles he takes on. He is not just an actor who plays parts, he is an actor who seeks out roles that challenge him, push boundaries, and bring attention to social issues. His performances in projects like "The Normal Heart", "Fellow Travelers", and "The Boys in the Band" reflect his desire to use his platform to tell stories that matter, ones that promote understanding, inclusivity, and acceptance.

But beyond his professional accomplishments, Matt's personal integrity and his commitment to family have cemented his place in pop culture. He is the embodiment of grace under pressure, someone who has managed to maintain his values and sense of self amidst the chaos of fame. His story is one of perseverance, passion, and authenticity, and it serves as a beacon for the next generation of artists, activists, and everyday people who seek to make a difference.

Through his advocacy, his acting, and his personal life, Matt Bomer has created a legacy that will continue to inspire. His story is one of a man who has never compromised who he is, who has used his voice to champion important causes, and who continues to evolve as both an artist and a human being. Matt's contributions to Hollywood, the LGBTQ+ community, and pop culture are immense, and his legacy will undoubtedly endure for years to come.

Made in the USA
Monee, IL
17 April 2025